MW00399280

The 7 Sins of Architects

Some wickedly accurate views about architects by **ROBERT ADAM** for *Building* magazine with illustrations by **LOUIS HELLMAN**

seven sins
CONTENTS

seven sins
INTRODUCTION

Architects are a funny lot. They're a mass of contradictions. They want the public to love them but despise the taste of ordinary people. They care about fine detail on buildings but don't take much interest in how they're put together. They want to be artists but are really just a service industry. They want to be moral and social reformers but have to work for dodgy politicians and cynical capitalists.

I've been a member of this profession for more than 35 years. I've been at the centre of its professional institution. I've been on official design review committees and judged numerous architectural awards. I've taught architecture and urban design. And I've been in private practice all this time.

My life in architecture is another contradiction. Although I'm close to the professional establishment, my designs are considered by many architects as not just in poor taste but also downright wrong. I'm what's loosely called a 'traditional' architect, that is, I design buildings that are recognisably descended from architecture that pre-dates the birth of modernism in the early twentieth century. This kind of architecture is very popular with the public and very unpopular with most architects.

This peculiar position has given me a combination of fondness for my fellow professionals and a cynicism about many of their aspirations and postures. I care about architects and architecture and, while I'd like these little essays to be the true word spoken in jest, they're intended to be positive. They're meant for non-architects as well as architects and I'd like them to be read by aspiring architects and students. Whoever you are, I hope you enjoy this little book.

Robert Adam, August 2010

" OH LOOK — ORDINARY PEOPLE ! "

the first sin: ELITISM

the first sin
ELITISM

When you walk into a room of architects, prepare for a fancy dress party. Some men will have suits with the lapels cut off, twenty cuff buttons, or weird colour combinations; you might see funny glasses (and even I'm guilty here), ethnic hats, or retro 80s student kit. You might be surprised to see sticking out the top of these curious costumes the familiar faces of comfortable well-off businessmen. Women, never really into business uniforms and more into fashion, look less like clowns but you will find the occasional bag lady and some scary makeup. It's a rather charming scene but behind it there's a serious message – architects are telling you that they're a tribe apart.

It's like the doctor's white coat and stethoscope or the barrister's wig and gown but, unlike doctors and barristers, architects go home in this stuff. The wacky get up is meant to tell everyone that you're interesting, creative and certainly not someone who could be described as run-of-the-mill. It's not just a way of saying that you don't look like the boring businessmen who pay you or the poor uncultured sods that have to live with what you do, it's a declaration that you don't want to be anything like them. If you're an architect you've joined an exclusive club and, like all exclusive clubs, it's worked out its own ways to keep out the riffraff.

Odd clothes are just part of the special members' recognition kit. There's the way of talking: doors are "entrances", windows are "glazing" and gaps are called "voids". If that doesn't work, there's where members live. This can be a bit tricky. Because they're fairly well off, they can buy the kind of high-status old houses that they don't think other people should copy. But if you can get inside it's a bit of a surprise, all the old stuff is stripped out and bare boards and very expensive, very uncomfortable chairs designed by founding members of the club are a dead giveaway.

Once you've joined the design professionals' club all that matters are the other members of your club.

Once you've joined the design professionals' club all that matters are the other members of your club. Success isn't the usual sort of thing like making money or being happy; it's measured by what other club members think about you. You've really made it when you get one of the prizes dished out by members to other members for being the best at sticking to the rules. And if anyone has a go at fellow initiates, members rally round to defend them. Defence groups are formed called "architects' panels" to make sure that the uninitiated don't have the brass neck to tell club members what to do. There are even ginger groups that think that there should be laws to make sure that only club members can do what lots of ordinary people want to do for themselves – design their own places.

Of course, keeping out the riffraff means that you're not interested in the riffraff. You may have to do things for the lumpen masses but it's not your job to give them what they'd like, it's their job to learn to like what you think they ought to have. There's even a special vocabulary for this – it's called "raising the bar" and doing it is called being "unapologetic", clearly in anticipation that someone's going to ask you to apologise. In fact, the declared mission of the club is to make everyone else want the same things that club members want. There are constant references to the great day when everyone is going to come round to their way of looking at things. Missions are sent out to persuade people in power to become associate members. This way, lots of people out there will get the "right" things even when they don't want them and this will force them to look up and see the true way. If all else fails, when they've had this stuff around for long enough they'll just get used to the idea and go along with it.

No one seems to have spotted the problem with all this. One of the best things about being a member of a club is that you're special and being special means that you're different. If everyone thinks and behaves like you, you're not different any more. The most important thing about being a member of an elite is to believe that you're superior and to do that you can't be like other people. Ordinary people will never be members of this club.

Published 17.04.2009

the second sin: CONCEIT

the second sin
CONCEIT

When architects are feeling down at the mouth, they pretend to be doctors. They don't go around asking people to cough or tap their knees, but they do claim some sort of moral high ground that they assume is occupied by the medical profession. Instead of being hated serial despoilers of people's treasured towns and cities, they want to be respected, important and above all they want everyone to think that they're ethical.

As most people don't like what most architects do, the friendly GP won't quite fit the picture. It's more "trust me I'm a doctor" as they amputate both legs. Architects will tell you that they must perform "radical surgery" on cities by cutting bits off and replacing them with shiny metal prosthetics. Or they will insist that they'll improve your "quality of life" by giving you minimalist shock treatment.

By imagining that they have taken some sort of aesthetic Hippocratic Oath, they fool themselves with the conceit that their fantastical schemes are really a dose of medicine for the good of a society. Sometimes they go so far as to claim that their sinister attempts at social engineering might actually save people's lives. Scared of being just the design department of the construction industry, they've created a monstrous delusion of self importance.

In the last few years a dream opportunity has turned up that allows architects to assume new heights of moral righteousness. Now they can claim not just to be curing social ills or rescuing aesthetically threatened lives, but to be saving the whole world. Delivering the planet from the unsustainable evils of the very development that is their stock in trade has become the new religion for the architectural profession. Not content with regulations and guidelines, they take on a moral duty to go one better. All sorts of sexy-looking eco-bling, that probably does the planet no good whatsoever, gets stuck onto buildings. Architects don't check if making it, transporting it and maintaining it cancels out any imagined benefits. The purpose is less to save the planet than to look good, make the architect look good and give a comforting glow of self-satisfaction.

Propping up this fantasy self-righteousness are high priestesses of smug who preach in professional magazines. A brilliantly circular doctrine of architectural morality as the path to true happiness is preached. The high priestess will tell you that she has been so virtuous with her designs that she has achieved divine joy. If you haven't been as virtuous as she then you can't be truly happy. You might be going along with the sad illusion that you're perfectly happy but you can't be because you haven't experienced the same levels of morally creative bliss. You won't know until you've got there and if you don't want to get there you'll never find out. There's no way out of this one.

But really we all know that architects are either businessmen or women pretending to be artists or artists who can't run a proper business. They do a job for money and do as they're told or they don't get any money and don't do the job. And there's nothing very ethical in architecture if you can't do any

architecture. The famous American architect Philip Johnson
got it about right when he said, "architects are prostitutes".
While they're ready to rubbish architecture of the past they
don't fancy just because a dictator happened to like it, today
ennobled architects do mega glass and steel jobs for some
pretty dodgy regimes and don't think twice. Architects'
ethics come from the chequebooks of their clients.

Architects' ethics come from the chequebooks of their clients.

Architects may have more in common with the oldest
profession than the medical profession but the doctor
delusion is not just more respectable it's much more
convenient. This way they can carry on doing pretty much
what they like, pretend that they know best about what's
good for society and then claim that they're not really doing
it for cash or ego but for the highest moral principles. It
doesn't matter if no-one wants it or likes it – and you know
it's good for them and you know you're good for giving
it to them. This is the perfect conceit.

But unlike doctors, architects don't wait for their patients to
come to them or ask them if they want to be cured. Of course
not, there's a good chance they'll tell you they don't want the
cure and, worse still, they might even tell you they're not ill.

Published 22.05.2009

GOLD MEDAL

the third sin: EGOTISM

the third sin
EGOTISM

How can you spot a genius when you see one? There aren't many about, so eliminating non-geniuses is a good start. To make it easier, if you find anyone who thinks they're a genius, you can be sure they're not. So, comic-book egg-head behaviour such as showy flashes of inspiration and telling everyone about your unexpected insights are not signs of genius – quite the opposite. You might have noticed that this is the way lots of architects behave. This means that, contrary to what they think of themselves, these architects aren't geniuses.

This shouldn't be a surprise. Most people aren't geniuses, so architectural geniuses will be very few and far between. The trouble is that architects are brought up to think that they're all great men or women in the making. Architecture schools have long abandoned the practical arts of knowing how to build, for which the seven-year-long course was designed, and largely devote themselves to things like making buildings look like magic mushrooms or discussing the finer points of broken tea pots. Any suggestion that time would be better spent getting the hang of how damp-proof courses work is dismissed as a needless impediment to the vital task of nurturing inspiration and genius.

Once you think you're a sage you can have a great time. All that matters is your inner voice. No longer do you need to pay attention to what people or your clients want. No, it's your job to find out what deep down they really want, not what the poor souls were naive enough to think they wanted. You needn't bother with dull stuff like working out how bits of buildings fit together. That's for dummies and a distraction from the real job of expressing the latest version of French philosophy with bent steel and pointed bits of glass. Best of all, not only are you always right but, if anyone says you're wrong, this just proves the point – ordinary people don't understand genius. An overlooked or persecuted master-mind is given a special place in the pantheon of unrecognised prodigies along with soon-to-be-discovered artists starving in garrets. Thinking you're above the rest is what makes egotists arrogant.

Thinking you're above the rest is what makes egotists arrogant.

Examples are not hard to find. Take the Scottish Parliament. If anything should be about the identity of the people of Scotland, this is it. But did Enric Miralles ask anyone in Scotland what they thought stood for their much-loved nation? Of course not, Miralles was a genius. Instead he took a quick trip round the place and found out what really made Scotland a special place – boats. Not any old boats but boats being made in towns, then being launched and going away. (You couldn't make this up, but believe me it's true.) So for generations to come MSPs will have to sit in what a Catalan who reckoned he was a genius decided was a typical Scottish decision-making place – an unfinished boat. A pity no one

16

in Scotland has the same idea. And what about the strange hairdryer-shaped seagull-nesting platforms fixed all over the building? Well, I can tell you the secret, they're a sort-of-but-not-quite silhouette of Raeburn's painting of the skating minister in the Scottish National Academy. Unlike the boats, Miralles didn't tell anyone about this. The poor people of Scotland, who paid a fortune for this mad composition, have to live for the foreseeable future with Enric Miralles' massive display of egotism.

Then there's the king of ego, Daniel Libeskind, who can decide that the real meaning of north London can be summed up with one of his architectural car crashes. In spite of the fact it's much like all his other built jumbles, his inner genius has decided that this is just the thing because lots of different people live there from all over the world. Or Foreign Office Architects who had the staggering insight that the identity of Birmingham was its sky – yes really. And this is why New Street Station will be wrapped in a huge curtain of reflective stainless steel which will reflect (wait for it) the sky – at least until it gets dirty.

We're increasingly stuck with what someone with a deluded idea of greatness thinks is the identity of our precious villages, towns and cities. Their ego tells them that their genius and inspiration is so much more important than the things we think connect us with the places we call home. Is it any wonder that many of us feel strangers where we live?

Published 07.08.2009

the fourth sin: DOGMATISM

the fourth sin
DOGMATISM

You might think that a laid-back, cool, smart-arse profession like architecture would be full of open-minded, up-for-debate, liberal dudes. Well, you'd be wrong. Don't even attempt a sparkling discussion about the pros and cons of structure and aesthetics unless you want to end up in a Punch and Judy show. Somewhere in the dark recesses of their educational past a rigid dogmatism was inserted into the soul of every architect. Buried in their breast is a deep conviction that knows no reason and brooks no challenge. Question this ineffable belief and expect a mouthful of rabid gobbledegook or just a sniffy silence.

This pig-headed behaviour perplexes many a poor client who's been foolish enough to think he or she has employed a rational being who may just like to discuss what the person who pays the bills might want.

But what is it that drives these fanatical ideologues? Above all, most of them believe with a passion that they were brought to this earth with a duty to save the poor misguided public from the imprisonment of their own taste. Being modern is not just something that happens because you're part of it, it's something you have to work at and, once you've got it, you've got to make sure that everyone else gets it – whether they like or not. This is not just taste or fancy, heaven forbid, it's a calling and a duty. If someone doesn't agree argument is pointless, it's action that counts. If they're a client, then they're just not offered anything else, however much they ask. If they're the public, they just have to put up with it.

This is so fixed amongst architects that whenever you see anything to do with new buildings published or talked about it's always the same kind of examples and illustrations that appear. If there's a book about houses, don't expect to see anything like the houses that most people buy, unless it's to poke fun at them. All the houses will be oddities, most of them built by architects for themselves, their family or their mates. And if anyone outside the magic circle goes along with all this they will become instant heroes and stand as "irrefutable evidence" that everyone's starting to fall in line and believe all this stuff.

Reserved for special disgust are the very few architects that don't toe the line. They let the side down and are in danger of letting the cat out of the bag by telling people that buildings don't have to be strange things they don't like. Giving Joe Public the idea that they can get what they want is very dangerous indeed. These people need to be kept out of the way and silenced wherever possible.

This little group of dissenters (let's call them the Traditionalists) are so battered and bruised by all this that they've created their own dogma. The key thing to their thinking is that anything the other lot (let's call them the Modernists) do is bad. So the Traditionalists define themselves by being what the Modernists aren't. The problem with this is that it puts the Modernists in charge in a negative sort of way. If the Modernists have an idea, the odds are the Traditionalists will think it's no good.

Of course the clever thing for the Modernists would be to think up lots of vaguely traditional ideas and push the Traditionalists into a smaller and smaller corner. Luckily for the Traditionalists the Modernists are so bound up in their own dogma that they'd rather boil their heads in oil than do anything that anyone might think belonged to the other side.

So architects are divided up into hostile camps. There are two main ones, one much bigger than the other. The Modernist camp has its own set of dissenting camps too but they all agree on the big issue – you must never be mistaken for a Traditionalist. And the Traditionalists have a matching principle – you must never be mistaken for a Modernist. This means that a good idea from one side never finds its way to the other.

Giving Joe Public the idea that they can get what they want is very dangerous indeed.

So while each camp works itself up into more and more fanatical ways of keeping the others out, it's architecture that suffers. And architecture is more about the people that live with it than the obscure ideas of those who design it.

I suspect that most people really would like something traditional and modern-looking but, the way it's going, architects won't deliver it.

Published 11.09.2009

"THEN WE WENT TO VENICE TO SEE THIS GREAT BUILDING BY FRANK LEE GHARISH "

the fifth sin: IGNORANCE

the fifth sin
IGNORANCE

If you're a bit of a local history buff and you meet an architect, you might want to have a chat about the old buildings in your area. There'll be lots of architectural things you'd like to find out about: the kind of columns on the manor porch; the date of some houses; what the decoration means on the church. Or you might just welcome the chance to talk to a fellow enthusiast. Be prepared for a disappointment. The odds are your new architect friend knows absolutely nothing about anything historic and what's more isn't that interested.

If you still want to chat to your new acquaintance about his professional interests, keep off architectural history and stick to things like the latest way of fixing titanium fins or whether solar panels can look sexy. For most architects, history starts in a small way around about 1930 and before that everything is irrelevant. It can even be dangerous because if they got to like old buildings they'd lose all their architect friends. Making sure you know nothing useful about what architects did in the past is not thought to be a handicap by architects today, on the contrary, it can be a duty and a badge of pride.

You'd think that, as most architects design in historic places sometime in their career, some idea of what old buildings are about might be a good idea. But what architects thought in the past is not what today's architects want to know – they're much more interested in finding some mystery proportion or obscure principle that only they can understand. And once they've found it, they can argue that any weird shape or odd collection of materials will fit in. It doesn't matter that no-one else can spot the great secret they claim they've discovered. Architects don't care if anyone else can understand what they're doing. They're just as proud of not knowing what the public think as not knowing anything about history.

> Architects don't care if anyone else can understand what they're doing. They're just as proud of not knowing what the public think as not knowing anything about history.

For architects, nothing is more annoying than public opinion. The trouble is that normal people care about building style and there's a serious danger that, if you ask the public, they might ask you to design something they like. Just in case this does happen, architects have already worked out a handy get-out clause. Each time the subject comes up you'll be told that, "what matters is quality, not style". This is a clever way of getting out of the problem but the real meaning is not quite what it seems. Saying quality matters is like saying virtue is good; it means nothing. So what this really means is just that "style doesn't matter". Which, of course it does. But saying it doesn't matter means, "I don't care what style you want, I'll design in my own style, thank you very much".

Of course, it's best to avoid the problem by not asking people in the first place. It's much easier not to know than to find out. If you know, either you have to take notice or admit you're not taking any notice. If you don't know, you can claim that the public do like it really, or that you think the public are coming round, or even that the public should like it and soon will if you give it to them. The last thing that architects want to do is to worry about what the people who have to live with their buildings actually want; this will get in the way of their artistic genius. They'd prefer to behave like an author who isn't interested in whether anyone's going to read their novel. Ignorance, after all, is bliss.

Although most architects don't know and don't care about what anyone other than their fellow architects think about their buildings, they do want to make sure that everyone can see them. This needs lots of space round the building and is called "public space", which sounds good but isn't. It's only public if the public use it and, often as not, it ends up bare, barren and dotted with little eddies of dust, crisp packets and newspapers. For architects, towns and cities are just big display cases for their work. The fact that the place matters so much more than the building is something else they just don't want to know. Making good cities is the last thing on their minds. As the heroic urbanist Jane Jacobs was heard to say, "the most cunningly ignorant people I know are architects."

BUILDING

ARCHITECTURE

the sixth sin: INCOMPETENCE

the sixth sin
INCOMPETENCE

The most important thing a building has to do is to keep out the water and weather. In fact, it wouldn't really be a building if it didn't. It also needs to take the rough and tumble of daily use and hold together pretty well for some time. It may surprise you to learn that these are the things most architects are least interested in. Ask an architect just out of college how a builder with a hammer and saw might put together the fantasy project that has just won him prizes. You'll be met with a blank stare. You might want to get quite technical and ask him or her how the water runs off the building's tricky corners and fancy shapes, how that big curvy thing can be made and brought to site or how to turn a damp-proof course around a corner. Don't expect an answer. There's a chance he or she will pick all this up in an office later but, as they're all trained to be super-stars, wasting too much creative time on this boring stuff will just get in the way of future fame. Better not to bother; practical stuff is for dummies.

The 20th-century history of the architectural profession is one long retreat from the business of building. The first thing most clients want to know is how much their building will cost – after all it's theirs and they're paying for it. So of course, the first thing architects decided was too boring for them was working out how much buildings cost.

Before the war they handed all that over to quantity surveyors. Next, all the poor unqualified grunts in their offices who really made sure the buildings could be built, stand up and keep out the water wanted some form of recognition. They formed an institute and called themselves Architectural Technicians (now Technologists) and made sure they had a proper qualification. Architects wanted nothing to do with this lower order and their Institute told them to go away. More recently, a new breed of experts turned up and called themselves Project Managers. Some of them were the Quantity Surveyors, who now had charge of the thing most clients worried about most – money. Some of them were builders, who knew that most architects didn't have a clue about what happens on a building site. Project Management sounds efficient and business-like but most of the time they're just doing what architects are supposed to do but often don't. So now, talking directly to clients, coordinating the team, running the job on site is all too often handed over to aggressive people who seem to take pleasure in being nasty to the architects whose jobs they've taken over.

What did architects do about this series of take-overs? Nothing. In fact, while they were at it, they let landscape and interior design get away. So what's left?

There's still working out how to fit functions into buildings. Sometimes that's quite complicated but most of the time it's pretty simple. Offices are just walls around open space, lifts and lavatories; factories are sheds without lifts and there aren't many new ways to plan a terraced house. Of course, there's still a lot of ways of getting the plan wrong. Think about public buildings with concealed pods that no-one but vandals want to visit. Think about museums that are only designed to show off the building, not the exhibits. Think about buildings so impractical that they have to be closed down almost straight away. Then think of really famous architects. If you care more about your reputation than the function of what you're designing, you'd think it was a formula for disaster. Not for architects it seems.

Architects who want to carry on being architects and want to be famous are left with making fancy shapes and thinking up really complicated reasons for making them odd and unbuildable.

Some architects get fed up with the whole nasty business of trying to design things that people want for a price they want to pay – it's so demeaning. They become social commentators, graphic artists or go into the new megalomania – master planning. Architects who want to carry on being architects and want to be famous are left with making fancy shapes and thinking up really complicated reasons for making them odd and unbuildable. They'd probably be insulted if we described them with the word Disney Corporation use for their designers' work – "imagineering" – but once the architect's technical know-how has gone, imagination is all that's left. Imagination is wonderful and we need it, but not everywhere all the time and for making buildings that don't leak it's not enough.

Published 26.02.2010

the seventh sin: PROFLIGACY

the seventh sin
PROFLIGACY

If you want to build anything much bigger than a house, you'll need an architect. You might think it would be a good idea to take on a big-name architect or at least an aspiring big name architect – which is pretty much the rest of the profession. And, unless you're a millionaire or mad, when you want a new building you'll watch your pennies. You might want the building to make you money. You might want to spend your savings on a pet project. And if you're the government, you'll be spending the hard-earned money you've taken off everyone else. Now, put these things together – your precious cash and an architect who thinks he should be famous – and you've got a problem. Pretty soon you'll worry that your special funds or your touch-and-go investment might just fall foul of an architect's devil-may-care attitude to building costs.

Self-important architects aren't really interested in their client's pockets except to make sure they get their fees paid. For them, buildings aren't really for their clients at all; they're for architects to show off to other architects. And the client's only there to go along with these fantastical exercises in ego inflation and pay up. After all, it's art isn't it? And it's the building that's left for posterity, not the client's overdraft. To quote a well-known architect on his overspend, "People should look at the architecture – that's what will be there in a hundred years."

This is the art-at-any-cost disease. The symptoms are easy to spot: ignoring budgets until the masterpiece is just about to be built; an unhealthy obsession with useless but expensive details and throwing toys out of the pram at the very idea of value-engineering. The disease is caught from the infectious idea that if architecture is art it must be tricksy, off the wall and have lots of fancy bits. For architects, there's no credit in a low-cost, simple and practical building. If it doesn't shout out people might not notice it and there's no reputation to be made in economy and modesty.

High-profile projects with big-name architects are notorious for running away with costs.

High-profile projects with big-name architects are notorious for running away with costs. After the grand-daddy of them all, the Scottish Parliament, the British Parliament didn't want to be left out but their offices couldn't quite come up to the standard of Edinburgh's 1,000% over-spend and they had to settle for 70%. Another symbol of Britishness, Wembley Stadium, checked in at £35 million over budget and then a symbol of British culture and history, Bath Spa, was notorious for costing an extra £32 million. Cultural buildings are often supposed to be made more famous by their star architects but can just become showcases for wasted money. Glasgow, always competing with Edinburgh, came up with an extra 50% at its last count (it's not finished) for its transport museum. The so-called "Public" in West Bromwich, (which the public don't go to) cost £12 million more than the original figure and the funny-shaped "Banana" in Colchester cost so much more than expected it was nearly abandoned. The biggest irony of all is that the Architecture Foundation, which spends its time promoting prima donna architects, engaged the star architect to beat all stars who managed to get to 100% over budget before work began and then they couldn't find a builder who'd build it. Of course, it's only fair to say that there's often more to the big-money overspends than architects going over the top but it's a bit too common to be just a coincidence.

These are all buildings designed by architects who are so famous that their buildings appear in all the magazines, win all the awards and are the heroes of students and wannabe big-names. The profession don't give awards to one another for coming within the budget or completing a building on time. On the contrary, many award winners are already notorious for wild over-expenditure and when architects hand out awards to their mates for over-priced scandals they're saying a big sod-you to the clients' budgets.

The fact that the idols of the profession are often the worst overspenders does the profession no good. Getting buildings to the right cost is complicated and hard work but there's no automatic link between good design and spending a fortune. The fact that fame in the profession too often goes to profligate show-offs is an insult not just to clients' pockets but to the thousands of hard-working architects who slog away to get good design into a low budget.

Published 14.05.2010

And another thing...

Two more blasts from
ROBERT ADAM originally
published in *Building* magazine

GREENWASH

Just about everyone knows we've got to change our way
of life to save the planet. Isn't it a bit odd, then, to find
architects doing the same stuff they've always done and
going around making out that they're the eco-warriors to
end all eco-warriors? Why is it that the same old glass-
walled boxes and tower blocks that were invented in the
energy-rich 60s and 70s can do the business for the energy-
challenged noughties? Architects have discovered the magic
of greenwash.

The big idea behind contemporary architecture was that the
"new century" (that's the 20th century of course – now the
old century) was all about the latest machines and inventions
and not much else. New was good, old was bad. Architects
have become so fixed on this idea that they believe that,
whenever a new problem comes along, something innovative
and scientific will turn up and solve it. And better still,
something innovative and scientific always looks pretty cool.
This is the "more gadgets" theory of sustainability. And what
a great theory it is. You carry on doing the same old stuff,
chuck lots of technology at it (preferably odd-shaped and
brightly coloured) and then claim the moral high ground.

Of course, you don't chuck the technology at it yourself.
There's a whole new greenwash industry to help you.

Top of the list are environmental engineers. Pay them enough and they can take pretty much whatever you want, triple glaze it, fill it with argon, put a special finish on it, mess about with water and waste, do something very complicated with figures that no-one will challenge without doing even more complicated figures, say it's super-sustainable and, lo and behold, non-engineers fall for it. As the engineers get their best jobs from the big-name architects who need to greenwash their very expensive buildings, they're probably not going to tell anyone what they really know – the whole thing would do much better if you just gave the building thick walls and made holes in them for windows.

...the whole thing would do much better if you just gave the building thick walls and made holes in them for windows.

There are notable exceptions such as Patrick Bellew of Atelier 10 and David Strong of Inbuilt (formerly the MD of BRE Environmental). But ranged against them are not only legions of engineers keeping mum but a new breed of public relations greenwashers. They'll write you a sustainability policy that no-one will use, they'll draw up meaningless pseudo-scientific diagrams that look good on the website and, if you want to push the boat out, they'll even tell you that glass is sustainable because you can re-use it – really. If you want to make people think you're sustainable, call in the greenwashers.

Behind all the reports, the gadgets that break down, the jazzy vents that keep the occupants awake at night and the silly little windmills that don't work is the elephant in the room: building anything uses up a lot of energy and most of that energy comes from fossil fuel. The logical conclusion from this is inescapable: keep what you've got and improve it if you can and if you have to build anything (and often you do) make sure it lasts a long time.

What makes a building last a long time is really quite simple. It needs to be robust and adaptable. Robust buildings are made of solid, low-maintenance and preferably local materials. Adaptable buildings are daylit, easy to subdivide and service and don't depend on machinery – like lifts and air-conditioning. In other words, they'll be solid, low and narrow. We're surrounded by buildings like this that have lasted for centuries. Today we can do the same thing and do it better - better insulated and better serviced. Building one of these every couple of hundred years is, by any sensible measure, more sustainable than building a new deep-plan, air-conditioned, high-rise, mastic-sealed monolith on the same site every thirty or forty years.

The trouble is that how long a building lasts isn't part of the low carbon measuring system. In fact, lots of important things aren't included. The whole zero carbon game is focused on what new buildings do, not on the natural lifespan of buildings nor on the life of the people in them. There's no accepted system to measure the energy locked in building products – embodied energy. And without an agreed measurement system greenwashers can have a field day. If the BRE can come up with the barmy idea that oil-based plastic windows get a maximum sustainability rating, just think what staritects and their greenwashers can do with tower blocks.

Published 26.09.2008

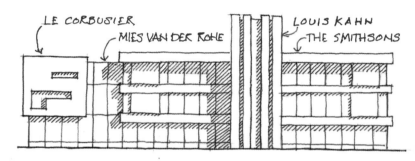

LE CORBUSIER

MIES VAN DER ROHE

LOUIS KAHN
THE SMITHSONS

A PASTICHE

Pastiche: Drawing by Author

PASTICHE

When architects want to rubbish traditional design they call it "pastiche". They roll out the 'P' word and think that one word is enough to damn it. It's so easy. But now, this mindless piece of architect's jargon has spread to the chattering classes and found its way into the planning system. When Bradford Metropolitan has a policy that says "new development must not resort to pastiche", when Hertfordshire stipulates that "proposals that provide a pastiche... should be discouraged", when someone senior in English Heritage announces that where "good modern design versus pastiche" there's "no contest", it's serious. When 'pastiche' is something officials want to stop, perhaps we ought to think carefully about what it means.

In the dictionary pastiche is "a composition made up of bits of other works or imitations of another's style". If this sounds bad, why? Sometime in the 20th century we got this strange idea that for art to be modern it has to be completely unlike anything that was done before. This is, of course, ridiculous. All art is based on ideas, influences and bits from other artists. In architecture, this applies to mainstream modernist as well as traditional architecture. Just how many new designs have glass walls just like Mies van der Rohe; how many architects use Corbusian curvy outside stairs or floating cubic walls?

Avoiding "imitation of another's style" would pretty well cancel out all architectural movements.

Avoiding "imitation of another's style" would pretty well cancel out all architectural movements. To avoid being "made up of bits of other works" architects would have to ignore every design feature by every previous architect. It would mean that you couldn't make an aesthetic nod to your hero and that you couldn't do something good because someone had already done it. This would not only be impossible; it would be stupid.

But the "pastiche" slander is reserved for new traditional designs. You might just avoid being condemned as a pastiche if you do a perfect copy - for some unfathomable reason exact replicas of historical buildings are often thought to be acceptable. But try and be creative with tradition and your work will be consigned to the special dustbin labelled 'pastiche'. And now, some ideological official can use written planning policies to make sure it stays in that dustbin and never sees the light of day.

But, except for a few periods such as neo-classicism, artists and architects of the past didn't make replicas but got their inspiration from different parts of history, mixed them up with ideas around at the time and made them into something new. Look at one of the most admired classical buildings of the nineteenth century, the Ashmolean Museum in Oxford.

Designed by CR Cockerell in 1839, the portico is from a 5th century BC Greek temple and a set of projecting columns and standing figures are from 1st century AD Rome. The whole thing sits on a rusticated base and is topped with a giant cornice, both taken from Italian Renaissance palaces. This is a pastiche if ever there was. Did this make all the critics, past and present, recoil? No, it did not and does not.

Then what about Foster's 1975 Willis Faber building: is this really Mies's 1922 glass skyscraper project with the top chopped off? Or Rick Mather's house in Hampstead: is this a thinly disguised 1997 rip-off of 1920s Corbusier? Then again there's KPF's up-and-coming Bishopsgate tower: is this weird glass spiral just a monster version of Vladimir Tatlin's 1919 Monument to the Third International?

So when is a pastiche not a pastiche? If we follow the definition properly, pastiche has nothing to do with style and, if we look closely, it applies as much to modernist as it does to traditional architecture. But when you're out to ban something you don't like, what's the truth got to do with it? "Pastiche" has just become a dumb shorthand that says "traditional architecture is bad" and "to be modern you have to keep reinventing the wheel". The first is bigoted and the second is pointless but traditionalists have learnt to expect nothing less. But when the government announce that they will be "giving good design the same status as sustainability" how will the bureaucrats interpret something as woolly as this? The bigots have already given them the tools. As Brighton and Hove have declared, "the plan seeks to raise the overall standard of design and encourage more innovative and distinctive design... pastiche designs will not be encouraged". This is code for "modernism good, traditional bad".